Louise Imogen Guiney

The Martyrs' Idyl, and Shorter Poems

Louise Imogen Guiney

The Martyrs' Idyl, and Shorter Poems

ISBN/EAN: 9783744771979

Printed in Europe, USA, Canada, Australia, Japan

Cover: Foto ©Thomas Meinert / pixelio.de

More available books at **www.hansebooks.com**

The Martyrs' Idyl

And Shorter Poems

BY LOUISE IMOGEN GUINEY

BOSTON AND NEW YORK

HOUGHTON, MIFFLIN AND COMPANY

The Riverside Press, Cambridge

1899

THE MARTYRS' IDYL

TO KATHARINE AND GILES

CONTENTS

THE MARTYRS' IDYL[1]

I

Sunset. A high rocky pasture above Alexandria. In the year of Our Lord 304.

Didymus, a young soldier, enters and throws himself down.

Didymus.

THIS mound is sweet to me. All my blood aches,
   Since driven onward like a dark hill-cloud,
Dizzy with secret lightnings nowhere spent,
I chase yon happy sun to his bright death,
Alas, I know not whither: but I know
I shall not see the myriad shields uphung
In camp to-night, nor on our cypresses
Smoke rise and sink in loath blue fountain spray.
So far, so far I drift from even them
Who fill one gourd with me, who cheer my heart,
Who come in, warm and singing, to the tent,
And miss me who am gone away, I think,
Forever, though a day; out of their world,

[1] The outlines of this story, and much of the dialogue, in Scenes II., IV. and V., are taken from the Acta Sanctorum and S. Ambrose.

Though over a few leagues of upland grass !
Why hast Thou laid on me magic of pain,
God unrevealèd ? Was I drawn from sleep,
Man's duty, body's health, to be mere wind,
Wind undirected over fallow wastes ?
What wouldst Thou ask of me, no sword of Thine,
No ark of service ?   Yet aware of Thee
I am and shall be.   All my thought, outspread,
Is open unto Thee : a lonely beach
Where the wide sobbing surf ebbs everywhere,
And, hard upon each dawn-encolored wave,
Flutters the wavy line of drying sand
Back to the verge : the white line, shadow-quick,
Thrilling there in the dark : an earthen gleam,
Vain huntress of the sea.   Suffer me now
To follow and attain Thee, fugitive,
And be my rest, who hast, my whole life long,
Been mine unrest : implored, immortal Love !

A Child *enters, with a reed, wearing a wreath of thorns in his hair.*

   The Child. Soldier, pipe up for me, a herd-boy,
      glad
Because his flocks are folded.
   Didymus.   Ah, not I !
My star is withered; I am man no more.
Sigh after sigh the builder Grief takes up,
To heighten over me her gradual arch.

The Child. An arch of entrance to a generous
    garden,
Where spirits and the moonlit waters are.
Take comfort !
    Didymus.   Thou art a strange child, methinks,
To say that too wise word.
    The Child.   Remember, then,
'T was breathed to thee at Alexandria,
In early-dying April's golden air.
    Didymus. Do I lie here, who deemed myself
    afar ?
I had forgot; I am foolish, lost, bewildered.
    The Child. O mine elect : be patient ! . . .
    Listen now.
There is an evening anthem in my reed ;
And while the laurels sparkle, and sun-lit,
The mother-swallow dips into her cave,
And doves move close along their bridal bough,
Murmuring sorrow, I will play to thee.
    Didymus. I thank thee, boy, for I may fall
    asleep.
    The Child. Rather shalt wake, and from thy
    doubt be born !
Lean so, against my knee.
                [The Child *plays, a long time.*
                O Didymus,
With thy shut eyes, thy youth undedicate,
Tell me the name of this new pastoral.

Didymus (*asleep*). He said : " My yoke is sweet,
     My burden light."
O light, O sweet, perchance, as it was said !
   The Child. True heart ! The hour rounds up ;
     thy wine-press waits ;
And so this music fades : the silver tones
Thin out, and faintly drip delight, and cease,
No willing man nor bird hears how. Good-night,
O soon-made-perfect !

II

Night. The same fields. Didymus *wakes, alone.*

Didymus.   It is black, and chill.
My little piper 's gone. . . . How I have dreamed,
How I have dreamed ! Lord, gather quietly
All wild hearts like mine own into Thy hand.
Yet on the look of these fresh-kindled stars
I feed, as if their bright benignant lips
Betimes had kissed the fever out of me,
And given to me their seat in warless air,
Their naked majesty, their poignant calm.
Not less remote my spirit, not less free,
After this unimaginable sleep ;
Having changed place, indeed, poor moth that was !
With vast abiding things : for now are cast
Old bonds, old ardors, expectation, ease,
Glory and death, belovèd land and sea.

Even as walled frost that feels the solar ray,
Curls up, impermanent, and reels far down
In long blue films, elfin, processional,
While the built stones fall to their first grave
          hue,
De-silvered : so the awful powers of earth
Exhale from me who stand the same; for these
Are vain, these are phantasmal, but not I.
At last I know myself, and know my need
As simply as a young child might, who cries
For honey from his father's liberal hive.
I will go down at dawn ; I will seek out
The Christian bishop, who shall lift me up,
A soul baptized. . . . Some lanthorn is beyond,
And moving.   Hail, there !   Would that I could
          say,
" The gods be kind to thee ! "
   A Voice.   And why not, friend ?
Thou greetest Cratidas, an old sad man,
On his home-going track.
   Didymus.   I too would house
A head as sad as thine : pause but a space ;
I 'll find thee on the road.   Now pray thee tell
Whose farms are these ?   His little herd-boy passed,
And spake or sang to me : Oh, if he were
An angel, or a Greater !
   Cratidas.   What art thou ?
   Didymus. One from the camp Nicopolis.

Cratidas.   I ask,
Leal to the State, or Christian?
  Didymus.   In this dark,
Imperial Diocletian's telltale dark,
And even to the sober ears of eld,
What danger in the word!   But now and here,
Danger I love as if she were my fawn.
Turn the lamp full this way : I 'll answer thee.
A true-accounted Christian I am not :
Afar from them my nurture; but I heard
How my young mother, long now in her urn,
Received them : whence aroma of their prayers
Haunted our dwelling ever.   In the wars,
I have been sick with longing and half-faith,
Last year and this ; that prickle has lived on,
Till every natural mirth is dead in me.
In the shunned name of Christ, I know not how,
Some harvest of mine innermost desire
Is sown, is springing up.   Art satisfied,
Father who servest Jove ?
  Cratidas.   Accursèd creed! —
Sir, there my hasty tongue spake for my heart.
A rebel girl I loved forsook me late,
Bit with the Galilean pestilence.
It rages, and it rots our best : be warned.
I am no spy ; I will befriend thee.   Come.
  Didymus. Thou livest nigh ?
  Cratidas. Not far.   Where yon sole gem

Swings from the new moon's girdle, is my hearth,
'Twixt grove and grove : a solitary place,
Since Theodora went.　　Hark !　. . .
　　Didymus.　　　　　　　　Sound of horror !
The city's anger must be under it.
　　Cratidas.　Ah me, I tremble : my poor lamb 's
　　　　the cause
Of such blind fury.　Bitter, is it not,
That her last kinsman, hearing, cannot help her ?
　　Didymus.　Cratidas, I would help !　Read pos-
　　　　sible aid
In this firm-sinewed arm.　Speak.
　　Cratidas.　　　　　　　　That I do,
As unto a well-wisher.　I distrust
Our fickle and tempestuous populace,
Greek, Roman, Jew, Egyptian, multiform.
Ah, the uproar !　I had not thought to find it
So fierce, so soon.
　　Didymus.　　　Speak quickly !
　　Cratidas.　　　　　　　　Loose my wrist.
Many light things are heavy to the old :
Therefore, let me not feel thy touch again,
The while I talk, and guide across the dew.—
I, weeping in the hall, some three days since,
Saw Theodora tried.　Aloft he sat,
Eustratius Proculus : no steely man,
But wise and gracious, in the prefect's chair.
I do not blame him.　(Mark the sudden gaps

Along our path.)   Eustratius Proculus,
The gold and purple fringing his white robe,
In a domed chamber, on a curving throne ;
And next the lighted jasper altar, wheeled
Far up the floor, boxed incense piled thereby,
Tall Theodora, like the lotus-flower
That rides a flooded stream ; lictors and priests,
Notaries, naked executioners,
Ranged thick about.   The prefect so began :
" Proclaim thyself."   " A maid named Theodora,
Ward of her aged cousin, Cratidas."
" What is thine age ? "   " They tell me, seventeen
        years."
" And thy condition ? "   Whereto she replied :
" Christ's."   Very patiently he asked :
" Art bond or free ? " as runs the rote of law.
She smiled in answering: " Free : made free by
        Christ ;
Else, of free parents honorably born,
Rhoxis and Heräis, who both are dead."
" Then why unmarried ? "   " For Christ's sake,"
        she said,
" I have been busied with the things of Christ : "
(For none could quench that hectic " Christ " in
        her,
Poor fool !)   Then spake Eustratius Proculus :
" Our code imperial deals with virgins thus :
Either unto the gods they sacrifice,

Or in an infamous place shall be exposed.
Come: one small grain within the brazier dropped,
And thou dost forfeit all pollution so,
Nor lose thy burial-rites." She, blanching not,
Looked up. "Thou art not ignorant, nor I,
How man's coöperate or revolted will
Doth color, in the councils of high Heaven,
Both what we do, and suffer. Violence,
Though sent to seek my soul, shall by her gate
Sit pilgrim-meek. Christ keeps His citadel."
The prefect bent again, compassionate :
" O girl ! rememberest not thy sires august ?
Pity thy beauty, heirloom of their house,
And precious most in thee. Choose to obey ;
Since even thee my duty cannot spare."
But she : " The nail-pierced Hands that have my
      vow,
Defend it." " Save thyself," he cried, " and trust
No crucifièd ghost. From foul disgrace
Snatch thine own youth." And she : " Behold, I
      do.
Christ is my source of honor, and mine end :
Christ shall be my preserver." Next I heard :
"Buffet her twice." Then: "Wilt thou sacrifice?"
My Theodora of the reddened cheek
Seemed absent from the body for a space,
Before she uttered: "No." " Child, I am grieved
For such affront, which all our city sees.

Thy quality invites another usage,
Wert thou not crazed." He paused, being full of
    ruth;
But self-relentless, she in that same pause
Brake forth : " O my one Wisdom, O my Joy ! "
And last, Eustratius Proculus rose up :
" The edict ! Let it work. I dally not,
For loyal and immovable regard
Unto mine Emperor." " Bid me stand as true,"
She murmured, " in allegiance to a Power,
Before whom sceptred Diocletian shines
Brief as this puffing coal." " Ai, blasphemy ! "
The vast crowd thundered. So they led her down
Into a three days' torture in the prison ;
And to the draped tribunal, all unchanged,
This eve she came. Said I, indeed, unchanged?
Her spirit and speech were that ; her body swayed
Hither and thither : a candle in a draught.
Some scrupled naught to praise such blithe disdain,
Immaculate, illumined ; who e'er knew
Disdain could wear a look so like to Love's ?
And thrice Eustratius Proculus read out
Sentence, whereby the virgin Theodora,
A Christian obdurate and impious,
Must die indeed, but first must be immured,
Until the day break, in the house of shame.
He ended : " May thy God for thee achieve
The best He can ! " She added : " Ay, He will.

As Daniel from the lions, from the deeps
Jonah; from furnace-heats the unbought three;
Peter from dungeon chains; as yesterday
Our Agnes from the Roman ignominy,
Shall I be rescued: He is faithful yet."
Softly she prayed: "Lord, Lord! deliver straight
Thy bounden servant, overshadowing
Thine own, in dread mid-battle, with Thy wing.
Out of Thy mercy, let them harm me not:
By thy most bitter Passion borne for man,
O Fount of chastity, O Fortitude
Of all Thy saints, Jesu! remember me."
Thus, in that voice which I shall hear no more.
I turned away, dragging my leaden limbs
Hillward, and homeward.
    Didymus.   And these shouts, these shouts,
Incessant, brutal, terrible, they mean —
    Cratidas. That now the lictors drive her forth;
    they mean
Quick menace to a never-soilèd blossom
Of Hellas come, and her heroic seed.
Ah, well: she will recant; she must recant. —
My young hound bays her welcome. Enter, sir. —
What! Gone? An armored man swooped like a
    hawk
Down the sheer ledges to the city's core?
Beware, my fiery nameless half-a-Christian,
Hot for romance, beneath the stars of spring!

Well, well, well, well! Down, Demo.   I believe
He 'll somehow free her: we shall have her back,
Good Demo. . . . Tut! of all the wild hawk-
    swoops!

III

Midnight.   A brothel.   Theodora *alone.*
Didymus *breaks in.*

Didymus.   Grant me forgiveness, lady Theodora!
And fear not.   I have spent my breath of life,
Beating the human hurricane outside,
To reach thee first of any.   Piteous thing,
Flutter not to and fro; thy net is cut:
No carrion crow shall ever prey on thee,
White dove! The evil room 's alive with light,
Thy light shed out; nor am I longer dark,
Who see, feel, bathe in it.   Oh, what a stream,
Full from within, as through a lattice door,
Widens around thee in an aureole;
From lifted eyes, loose hair, and hands unlocked,
Gushes the even glory!   While I look,
So bright, thou seraph of the golden blood,
Rains that pure fire on me, that now I know
Of what clear essence thou, not less am I;
Yea, I with thee, and all my thoughts with thine,
Run up before our God in one straight flame.
Child, I am here to help thee : Didymus,
A Cappadocian.

Theodora.   Heaven be thanked, and thou,
For I believe thee ! Cappadocia :
Was it not there the blessed Dorothy
Brought apples to her lover, after death,
In token of the riches of that orchard
Where Christ walks with His own ?   Let us go
    thither.
Didymus. Ah, muse no more.
Theodora.   The Lord abide with thee !
Didymus. Though unto me thy voice be like the
    foam
Upon a wave of quiet, thy delay
Dearer than wine of roses, rouse thee : haste !
How else can I the pact maintain with Him
Who bade me loose thee from the snare ?   Come
    nigh :
Doff thine apparel ; put mine armor on.
Think but of flight, and safety.
Theodora.   Wingèd one,
Best brother, brighter than a star, and stronger,
Uphold me !
Didymus. Bind thy locks.   Alas, I am
No angel sent of Christ, nor yet a Christian.
Theodora. Why dwell in lowland shadow ?
    Thou, ere long,
Must drink of grace divine the deathless light.
On, happy soul : for there are hills to climb,
E'en Calvary hill.

Didymus.   Art thou not vested yet?
The minutes seethe and rush. Oh, had I time,
I'd tell thee of my pangs: how it has been
From march to march with me; how vehemently
The sluices brake in this tormented heart,
Last night, ten lives ago; how on yon heights
A boy, (not sweeter Hyacinthus was,)
Having a pensive garland of green thorns
Intrailed among his auburn curls, came by,
And with his new-cut reed, and myrrhy lip,
Entranced me into slumber; how I saw
Thy foster-father, and walked on with him,
And heard thy sacred story: thence I sprang
Into this hell, where I for thee shall answer.
And do thou plead with Christ, for me His thrall.
    Theodora. The thong: pray knot it! Gentle
        Didymus,
Here is my robe: the stuff is torn; the stains
Began 'neath sharpened spikes, the hooks, the
        rack.
    Didymus. For dress of mine, good in the foray
        once,
That keeps thee and a holy dream intact,
Thou giv'st me this, strangely to make of me
The athlete of thy Lord. Well, give it so:
I kiss each dear and venerable stain,
And lay the rended linen over me:
Would I were worthier!

Theodora.   Cratidas the fond
Has somehow faded from me, and our roof
Among the date-palms, and my dial old,
Set in the myrtle plot that takes the sun.
But thou art close and real : thou hast seen
The Mystical, the Virgin-born : his name
Not Hyacinthus, but Emmanuel.
(Much have I startled thee, who art so brave !)
None shared with me that vision until now.
It was to Him I pledged my early troth,
Towards whom I live, for whom I look to die;
Whose love was sovereign healing unto me,
When late within the torture-cell I lay.
His chosen other, kneel not thou to me !
There is a Hand that will not let thine fall,
As mine doth.

    Didymus.   Sign me slowly with the cross.

    Theodora. So: on predestined brows.

    Didymus (after a pause).   Thy sandal's fast,
The breastplate firm and fine, each joint in place;
Draw low the vizor; let the short cloak hang;
And stoop in issuing forth: step hurriedly,
As one ashamed, whom his loud sins pursue.
Go thus, secure.

    Theodora.   Thou shalt not always hunger !
O thy requital: might I see it !

    Didymus.   Go :
Go, even as I said.

Theodora.   I am so weak :
What if I cannot ?
   Didymus.   Hush : unbar the door,
And front the pack. — My sister, my twin-born,
Live thy sequestered life ; and pray for me.

                              [Theodora *goes.*

Ah, gracer of our Roman mail !   I hear
No smallest rumor that her passage makes,
Not one least vicious snarl or jeer the more.
I dare to dream Thou hast accepted this,
My true task in the world ! By now, I think,
She leaves behind the fetid neighborhood ;
A moment more, and her accustomed feet
Will be among the vineyards and the folds.
The little weary feet wounded for Thee,
Do Thou sustain ! . . . They come.

IV

*Midnight.   The city square outside.   Didymus in the
   arched doorway of the same house.   A turbulent
   crowd around.*

   The Bailiff.   Give way, give way !
Order among ye, subjects, citizens ;
Order, I say !   A seaman, in this dark,
Would swear he heard the angry equinox
Gorging and emptying the island caves :
A swash of death, where he had hoped for haven.

Whence the commotion, that, from well-earned
    beds
Untimely drags your rulers? Ibrahim,
Or Rufus, any of you with unslit tongue,
Speak!
  A Voice. At me that am terror-struck they laugh,
Who was the first to find him : Come, mock not
Too easily, but measure what I saw!
I heard, and ye too heard, in likelihood,
What I called fable, that this Christian God
Changed water into wine ; yet in night's eye,
A slim maid that was shut 'twixt four known
    walls,
Your Christian God turns to a brawny youth,
Whom seven men and myself barely haled hither.
  Didymus. Murmur not, wonder not: ye are broad
    awake.
No trick hath been, nor am I one transformed.
Whom late ye thought to have, lo, ye have lost ;
And whom ye have unwitting, ye may keep.
There is a twofold glory on the hour :
A virgin is a virgin still, and I,
The empire's soldier, champion of her King.
  A Voice. A generous comedy!
  Another Voice.   Dost applaud it? Ay?
  The Crowd. See him in the doorway, yellow-
    gowned ;
See the young beauty in his flower! O Pan!

The Bailiff. Among these loud boors press your
    torches in.
Back!   Let the prefect pass.

Eustratius Proculus *is borne into the square.*

A Voice.   Now shall we view
The snorting tiger-dam at bay, the while
The cub's concealed.
    The Prefect.   Be silent!   Clear with rods
The threshold of that house: the accused alone
Shall stand there.   Hither and together call
The trumpeters, for I this cause arraign
In open air.

                              [*The trumpets sound.*
            Who so disturbs the streets,
With the grave ends of justice interferes,
And draws contempt on me?   What roysterer,
What prince of Alexandria's worst?
    Didymus.   I think
It must be Christ Himself, or Christ in me,
Since in His quarrel I stand ambushed thus.
    The Prefect. His talk is echo.
    The Bailiff.   Learned of lady-love!
Dull matter all: sheep filing over bars,
One hobble without end.
    A Voice.   Thy Theodora —
    Didymus. Revere that name; for she is Christ's
    alone,

Not mine, not mine. Whithersoever goes
The Lamb in Heaven, such do follow Him.
   The Prefect. Enough: with quick straight-
      forward words respond.
Who art thou, chief in this unseemly brawl?
   Didymus. One new to camp and city, one in-
      deed
No alien, but your servant in the wars,
Beneath the imperial eagles now three years:
Octavius Didymus, centurion.
   The Prefect. A Roman, then. What of thy
      friend, the woman,
Duly condemned for heinous sacrilege?
   Didymus. The innocent Theodora is set free.
In as a thief came I who gave such good,
But never greeted her, nor saw, nor heard,
Up to our late accost in this vile pen.
   A Voice. How now, neighbors? A joker.
   Another Voice.   Or a liar.
   The Crowd. More like, a fellow-Christian.
   Didymus.   Why a Christian?
   The Prefect. If not a Christian, it rejoiceth me,
Aweary grown of all the casuist breed.
I deem thou art sincere. The charge is light;
The penalty shall therefore too be light,
Since thou thyself of prior circumstance
Wert plainly unaware; and forasmuch
In thy regard, our judged idolatress

THE MARTYRS' IDYL
THE MARTYRS' IDYL
THE MARTYRS' IDYL

Was one with any whimsied wench, cajoling
A frolic hand to let her out o' doors.
   Didymus. Let us not fail in truth: sir, I knew
     this.
My soul's defiance glowed in all I wrought.
   A Voice. By Pompey's certain pillar, he's a
     Christian!
The prancing gesture, see: the head upcast,
The bosom all in a white wrath, and yet
Bridled and bitted: that's their duplex way.
   The Prefect. I hesitate.
   The Crowd.   Eustratius Proculus,
We take him for a Christian!
   The Prefect.   Prisoner,
Attend, and ease our cares. Obediently
Unto the known gods wilt thou sacrifice?
                 [Didymus *is silent.*
Art thou a Christian: nay?
   Didymus.   Tell me.
   The Prefect.   Alas,
Why loath to sacrifice? Do thou but so,
Irreverence to the law shall be condoned,
And for the brave adventure of a night,
No tax be laid.
   Didymus.   I sacrifice no more.
Who hath inspired me? I can but attest
One Infinite loved her for her confident eyes.
Would we were open to the heart of things!

For if He keeps without spot, as some say,
Those leal to Him, is it not wonderful?
And Him thus fair reputed, Him untried,
Shall I reject? I sacrifice no more,
Save to the Living: save to Him who died,
And rose again.
    The Bailiff.   Ye hear.
    A Voice.   A leprous word!
    The Prefect. It is a difficult hour: I must com-
      port
Myself within mine office, steadfastly.
Bring me the writ. One act is mine to do:
Another time for fond alternatives!
Though fain to spare, fain to respect in thee,
Arms, broadening empire, and invincible Rome,
I that would never, fighting civic harm,
See Diocletian fail, nor have it said
Great Decius and Valerian failed before,
Rise to the common weal, and so bar out
Contagion from our long inviolate air.
    Didymus. I feel the little lovely kiss of death
Breathe at my temples, softer than a bride.
    The Prefect. Octavius Didymus, bound in triple
      cords,
Shall be at sunrise, on the appointed plain,
Beheaded. Gracious Cæsar, hail! all hail!
    The Crowd. Hail, Cæsar!
    Didymus. These have made me Thine, O Christ!

The Prefect. Reflect: I can revoke, I would
    revoke.
Name but thy young confederate's hiding-place.
    Didymus. I know not, sir, where Theodora is.
She passed: and I remain. . . . Demonic laughter!
I would I had said less: it saddens me.
In all this swarm, there figures verily
Not one that will believe; not one kind soul
But is so sodden with the slime of life,
(Life pagan, and without our Star,) that he
Must read awry, and slander my fair deed.
Ah, if they knew: but wherefore should they
    know ?
Lord, fold amid the leafage of my heart
Her lilied memory! I will strive no more ;
But turn to Thee, away from time and tears,
A melting snowflake in Thy mercy's sea.
    The Prefect. Disperse.

                [*The trumpets sound.*
    A Voice.   Our novel damsel, fallen dumb,
On the good public flint shall soon strike fire ;
And we may trap that masking man-at-arms,
Before a lizard gets his inch of sun.
Ho, ho! Away: lead on !
    The Crowd.   Huzza ! huzza !

V

Dawn. The place of execution, west of the city, looking seaward. The same crowd, leading Didymus.

A Voice. A long march is well ended. How
    fares he ?
The Bailiff. He thrives ; I hear him murmuring
    idle spells.
Didymus. Soft is the twilight breeze, soaked full
    of sea.
The veiled isle yonder rears her breathing lamp ;
And under us, in hollows of the crags,
Each washing wave goes like a gentle gong.
Across the hills, there brims a lucent tide,
Inaudible, yet lovelier ; living gray
Ridges the pulsing east, a surf of light ;
And doubling ever on itself, a glow
Now near, now far, breaks up the crested sky,
As children, pink against the green sea-garden,
Play in the earthly waters, unafraid,
And ruddier than all roses, race ashore.
So come, so come, gracile and glorious,
O rose unborn, my Day !
The Bailiff.   We 'll halt awhile,
And shortly see our way to honest work. . . .
Listen ! Do others follow us, or no ?

It seemed our concourse emptied all the town.
Who stirs through this dim weather?

A slave rushes in.

A Slave.   Theodora!
They are bringing Theodora here to die.
  The Crowd. Victory!
  Didymus. Lord my God, what hast Thou wrought?
I tremble with the sorrow and the joy.
The shouts, the trampling feet, renew for me
A sacrifice I thought to make no more.
  The Bailiff. Drag her yet nigher.
  The Crowd.   She is welcome!
  A Woman.   See:
Her knees are white; the gold hair brushes them;
The glimmering breastplate, in the breaking dark,
Shows comely.
  A Voice.   Take it off!
  Theodora.   Not so; not yet.
  The Bailiff. Then tell thine own night's tale:
    there's privilege.
  Theodora. A simplest tale.   When dedicated
    hands
Gave me this dress, lest I should suffer wrong,
The strong disguise bred courage; but I went
Only a mile: the armor was too heavy.
Where blossomed almonds shade the roadside well,
Did I fall down, aswoon; I think I swooned
For long; and some late revelers, passing by,

Found me, and with a tumult took me hither.
Fulfill your will in pity; I would rest.
   The Bailiff. Half of the warrant drawn for Didy-
      mus,
Is yet to read: thy fate and his are one.
   Theodora. On Didymus? Most miserable I,
If he must suffer, being kind to me!
What have ye done with Didymus?
   Didymus.   I am nigh.
   Voices. Look: they have run together! Miscre-
      ants!
   Theodora. O strange ordaining! Tell me: by
      what right
Art thou encountered on the fatal ground?
   Didymus. By right more fair than thine, because,
      forsooth,
Not punished for thy planned deliverance,
But rather for the sacred Name, I stand
Thus ready to the headsman. Aye: give thanks;
Yet thou, too rash, hast clouded my last hour.
Did I not guard thee? Was my prayer in vain?
For into horror's mouth thou hast returned.
   Theodora. Nay: chide not. Test their changed
      intent, and mark
That in it lurks for me no word but " Death,"
No word at all but dear dispassionate " Death."
Were I, still helpless, in dread peril caught,
To thy releasing hand I still had cried,

Who could not yield mine honor up ; but this,
The debt of life, I can myself discharge.
And if I die not so for Christ, to-morrow
Will these be angered less with me ? and then
For taking flight, for guiltiness of thy guilt,
My helper, shall I not less nobly die ?
Was it from martyrdom erewhile I ran,
Or only from the maw of wickedness ?
And lightly I relinquished unto thee
My girlish raiment, not my soul and self :
My fond profession of the Christian name.
Would he deprive me now of my last due,
Greatly deceives me one I thought my friend !
What will become of me if thou shouldst go,
Alone ? That cruel hour would strike away
My second sentence, glad, desirable,
And lower me to the insupportable first.
Leave me not to the torment ; rather share
The blessedness ; be jealous even for me !
Let it forevermore of thee be told
How from the thousand hands of a brute foe
Thou savedst once the spouse of Christ for Him.
Ah, Didymus, Didymus ! of the eternal crown
Rob me not thou : for thine to thee I gave.

 Didymus. Thy sovereign pinion overmasters
  harm,
Life, Death, and me : and if I feared, I erred.
We shall not be divided : and therefore

Blessèd be One who hath despised me not,
And, of His clemency, absolved from ill
His handmaid Theodora.
   Theodora.   Blessèd He,
Towards only children twain, most merciful
Both in the olden time, and unto us,
Who so, in triumph, wait our vigil's close.
O Light from Heaven, break, break!
   The Bailiff.   Attend, all men :
Heed how to deal with perished Christian swine,
For much the law doth vary, touching them.
And since, too oft, their kind do set a watch,
And, ere the wild beasts from their lairs descend,
Conceal their bodies elsewhere, 't is decreed
That these upon the bordering desert straight,
Shall, after death, be burned.
   The Crowd.   It suits us well.
   Theodora. Then not to secret chambers of the
        rock,
Our own, with hymnal rite, shall lead us home ;
Not to our natural nest beside the sea,
Above blown Pharos and the trader's sail,
Where, day and night, the Eucharistic Love
Broods over us, shall thou and I be borne,
And laid amid our fathers in the Faith,
Sleep the good sleep of immortality.
Not one small tress of ours shall reverence save ;
No fragment of our interchangèd garb

Be shrined forever, nor ascetic lips
Embrace, in our carved names, the Crucified.
God's Will be done, and done with all accord
In all ! and may He grant that unto thee,
(Who art both more and less than neophyte,)
Denial of that quiet sepulture
Be not so keen a pain.—His look 's afar:
He has not answered.

    Didymus.   . . . Whole on every side !
Whole, boundless, and immingled : not a chink
In tremulous textures of this bubbly world,
Where spirits might slip through. O spacious
      hour
Of ocean-distances, air-altitudes,
Pearl cloudless rounding over waveless pearl :
Pure Mediterranean ! bland Africa !
Ignoble are the dreams that make of you
Mere ante-room ; and ante-room to — what ?
True to original and terminal earth,
Rather may royal man, ensphered so fair,
His chemic end not thanklessly salute,
When too soon, from our arc of known content,
We blunder, poor blithe faces, to the Void.
That spark once fallen, can it live again ?
If poets weep, if just Aurelius
Evade, if wistful Plato pause unsure,
Ah, who art Thou that biddest me believe ?

    Theodora. Encased in thy so serviceable steel,

Against my bosom, I have kept for thee
An aromatic and a covered cup.
Come hither: drain it.   Sudden over me,
While I lay stricken, ere my captors came,
There bent the childish Shepherd of the hills,
Austerer than his wont, and uttered low:
"Wake, Theodora! Bear to Didymus,
Whom, spent in final battle, thou shalt meet,
A little draught of mingled wine and dew,
For baptism, and viaticum."

   Didymus.   I hear.
A stupor, a temptation, clogged my brain:
Gone evermore. — What hast thou been to me!
In any of God's halls where I may find Him,
I seek thee also there: O dove! thou knowest
Thy hidden heavenly way through words withheld.
I kneel, but cords impede my hands.   Pour thou,
Till I have slaked a supersensual thirst,
And, faint with salutation, drink to Him,
Christ Jesu, whom in dying I adore.

   The Bailiff. Despatch: broad daylight comes.
   The Headsman.   All is prepared.
   Theodora. Amen: and Alleluia! Heart flown
      home,
If thou wouldst speak, rise up.
   Didymus.   Ye worthy men,
I would not stay you long.   Of Didymus,
Who made his port of intellectual storm

At Alexandria, tell only this :
That he for Christ died Christian, with clear joy.
And when his comrades from their outpost ride,
And, reining in abreast, ask news of him,
Lay in their wondering ears, I charge you all,
That word miraculous, that happy word.
   A Voice. I ever knew it.   Devil! Sorceress!
   The Bailiff. What troubles them?
   The Crowd.   The bowl whereof he drank,
Between her lifted fingers melts away!
Their magic arts, and them, destroy!
   The Bailiff.   The axe :
Smite first the soldier.
   Didymus.   Theodora saint,
How beautiful, how more than banner-bright,
Streams over the far roofs our birthday sun !
Farewell, and follow me.   [Didymus *is executed.*
   The Crowd.   Blood! blood! The other!
   Theodora. Each moment of mine exile, so dis-
         tinct,
So vast, so bitter, and so ever-during,
Burns sweet before Our Lord: love's last slow
         grain
Rich as the first : for lo, the censer's broken;
And all my soul foreruns her call to climb
Out of this ruin.   Lest I slip, or cry,
O visible form of light, dear Didymus!
Turn now : give me thy hand.

SHORTER POEMS

THE SQUALL

WHILE all was glad,
  It seemed our birch-tree had,
  That August hour, intelligence of
    death;
For warningly against the eaves she beat
Her body old, lamenting, prophesying,
And the hot breath
Of startled ferny hollows at her feet
Spread out: a toneless sighing.

Across an argent sea,
Distinct unto the farthest reef and isle,
The clouds began to be.
Huge forms 'neath sombre draperies, awhile
Made slow uncertain rally ;
But as their wills conjoined, and from the north
The leader shook his lance, O then how fair
Unvested, they stood forth,
In diverse armor, plumed majestically,
Each with his own esquires, a King in air !

Up moved the dark vanguard,
With insolent colors that o'erdusked the skies,

And trailed from beach to beach:
Massed orange and mould-green; vermilion barred
On bronze and mottled silver; saffron dyes,
And purples migratory,
Fanned each in each,
As the long column broke, athirst for glory.

Sudden, the thunder!
Upon the roofed verandas how it rolled,
Twice, thrice: a thud and flame of doom that
      told
New-fallen, nor far away,
Some black destruction on the innocent day.
And little Everard
Deep in the hammock under, eyes alight
With healthful fear and wonder
The brave do ne'er unlearn,
Clenched his soft hand, and breathing hard,
Smiled there against his father, like a knight
Baptized on Cressy field, or Bannockburn.

A moment gone,
Into our Thessaly, from Acheron,
With imperceptive sorcery, crawled ashore
Odors unnamable: an exhalation
Of men and ships in oozy graves. (Ah, cease,
Derisive nereids! cease:
Be it enough, that even ye can pour,

From crystal flagons of your ancient peace,
So strange obscene libation.)
But with the thunder-peal
Sprang the pure winds, their thuribles swung wide,
To chase that tainted tide;
Fresh from the pastures and the cedar-grove,
They rode the ridged Atlantic's copper plain,
And rent a league of distance to reveal
A sail, aslant, astrain,
Impetuous for the cove;
And tossing after, panic-stricken,
Another, and a third : white spirits, fain to sicken,
Nor out of natural harm salvation gain.

The selfsame hunter winds that drave
The horror down, as faithful-hearted drew
The sad clouds from their carnage, and up-piled
Their rebel gonfalons, or jocund threw
Their cannon in the wave;
And subtly, with a parting whisper, gave
An eve most mild :
A sunset like a prayer, a world all rose and blue.

A good world, as it was,
And as it shall be : clear circumferent space,
Where punctual yet, for worship of their Cause,
The stars came thick in choir.
Sleep had our Everard in her cool embrace,

Else from his cot he hardly need have stooped
To see, (and laugh to see !) the headland pine
Embossed on changing fire :
For close behind it, cooped
Within a smallest span,
In fury, up and down, and round and round,
The routed leopards of the lightning ran :
Bright, bright, inside their dungeon-bars, malign
They ran; and ran till dawn, without a sound.

MEMORIAL DAY

DAY of roses and regret,
Kissing the old graves of our own !
Not to the slain love's lovely debt
Alone;

But jealous hearts that live and ache
Remember, and while drums are mute,
Beneath your banners' bright outbreak,
Salute:

And say for us to lessening ranks
That keep the memory and the pride,
On whose thinned hair our tears and thanks
Abide,

Who from their saved Republic pass,
Glad with the Prince of Peace to dwell:
Hail, dearest few ! and soon, alas,
Farewell.

ROMANS IN DORSET

TO A. B.

STUPOR was on the heath,
And wrath along the sky;
Space everywhere; beneath
A flat and treeless wold for us, and
darkest noon on high.

Sullen quiet below,
But storm in upper air!
A wind from long ago,
In mouldy chambers of the cloud, had ripped an
arras there,

And singed the triple gloom,
And let through, in a flame,
Crowned faces of old Rome:
Regnant o'er Rome's abandoned ground, proces-
sional they came.

Uprisen as any sun
Through vistas hollow grey,
Aloft, and one by one,
In brazen casques the Emperors loomed large, and
sank away.

In ovals of wan light
Each warrior eye and mouth:
A pageant brutal bright
As if, once over, loudly passed Jove's laughter in
    the south;

And dimmer, these among,
Some cameo'd head aloof,
With ringlets heavy-hung,
Like yellow stonecrop comely grown around a
    castle roof.

An instant: gusts again,
And heaven's impacted wall,
The hot insistent rain,
The thunder-shock; and of the Past mirage no
    more at all.

No more the alien dream
Pursuing, as we went,
With glory's cursèd gleam:
Nor sins of Cæsar's ruined line engulfed us, inno-
    cent.

The vision great and dread
Corroded; sole in view
Was empty Egdon spread,
Her crimson summer weeds ashake in tempest:
    but we knew

What Tacitus had borne
In that wrecked world we saw ;
And what thine heart uptorn,
My Juvenal! distraught with love of violated Law.

VALSE JEUNE

ARE there favoring ladies above thee?
    Are there dowries and lands? Do
      they say
Seven others are fair? But I love
    thee:
      Aultre n'auray!

All the sea is a lawn in our county;
    All the morrow, our star of delay.
I am King: let me live on thy bounty!
      Aultre n'auray!

To the fingers so light and so rosy
    That have pinioned my heart, (welladay!)
Be a kiss, be a ring with this posy:
      Aultre n'auray!

A LOYAL lady young; a knight for honor slain :
All beauty and all quiet sealed for aye upon
Their images that lie in coif and morion.
A moment since, through rifts and pauses of the rain,
The day shot in; the lancet window showered again
Its moth-like play of silver, rose, and sapphire; shone
What arms of warring duchies glorious, bygone :
Lombardy, Desmond, Malta, suitored Aquitaine !
The while aloft in Art's immortal summer-tide,
Fair is the carven hostel, fortunate either guest,
And men of moodier England pass, and hear outside
Fury of toil alone, and fate's diurnal storm,
Hearts with the King of Saints, hearts beating light and warm !
To these your courage give, that these attain your rest.

MONOCHROME

SHUT fast again in Beauty's sheath
    Where ancient forms renew,
The round world seems above, beneath,
    One wash of faintest blue,

And air and tide so stilly sweet
    In nameless union lie,
The little far-off fishing fleet
    Goes drifting up the sky.

Secure of neither misted coast
    Nor ocean undefined,
Our saddening sail is like the ghost
    Of one that served mankind,

Who in the void, as we upon
    This melancholy sea,
Finds labor and allegiance done,
    And Self begin to be.

THE VIGIL IN TYRONE

TO G. S.

ELL it over!" Thus, in twilight, the
old gamekeeper of gentle blood,
To the grandchild teasing, teasing, and
pink as the bedtime daisy-bud,

Tells it over.— "When that happened, I was a boy,
and I sat one day
By the river, in mid-morning, my drowsy cheek to
the pleasant clay.

"Sudden opened, near and under, the believed-in
cave on the green hillside!
Thick the darkness, but I saw them: the Earl
Hugh's men that never have died,

"Men gone by, ensainted, fabled, the men unnamed
in the living air:
Like a taper's flame among them, my soul and
body were shaken there.

44

" Nine full hundred, nine and ninety, (O'Neil the
  thousandth when he comes back !)
All a-row, asleep in armor, by horses magical white
  or black :

" Mighty horses satin-shouldered, with sheen of the
  golden stirrups grand ;
Mighty troopers drunk with battle, the bridle in
  every iron hand.

" Sunburn on their folded faces was fresh as child-
  hood and fierce as death.
Think : the sunburn got in marches against the
  demon Elizabeth !

" Next my knee, then, rose a hero, rose up a little,
  not loosening rein ;
Gazing steady, softly said he, and sharply said to
  me, over again :

" ' *Is the time come?* '   (That's for vengeance : the
  clan is hungry and hot to start.)
' *Is the time come, is the time come?* '   Thrice the
  sound of it stabbed my heart.

" Page or herald if he thought me, the hope that
  changed like a rushing sea,
Failed and ebbed, and straight outbore him, and
  took the terror away from me ;

" Sands of sleep dragged down his eyelid, and slacked
          his hand on the charger good,
Surely,   heavily,   surely,   slowly. — I   ran   till   I
          reached our roof in the wood.

" Long ago.   This thing the fathers had whispered
          of, I beheld and heard !
Though not yet my splendid dreamer the answer
          win to his uttered word,

" Patience : that shall be, hereafter.   The chief is
          late, but he seeks his own,
Riding up to break the quiet in all the farm-lands
          of all Tyrone.

" They have hid so, they have waited ; to hate that
          smoulders their blood is leal.
O to help them crash around him true Innishowen's
          unrusted steel !

" O to help them cheer and follow O'Neil, O'Neil
          from his foreign grave !
O to throne thee, saddest, fairest, as once thou
          wert, on the warless wave !

" Drift of moss for many a summer conceals the
          door on the charmed hillside ;
Clouds and hail of death blow over the Earl Hugh's
          men that never have died.

" Nine full hundred, nine and ninety, (O'Neil the
 thousandth when he comes back!)
Lie a-row, asleep in armor, by horses magical white
 or black:

" Mighty horses satin-shouldered, with sheen of the
 golden stirrups grand;
Mighty troopers ripe for battle, the bridle in every
 ready hand.

" ' Is the time come? '   (Long the sorrow, little isle,
 my love, for your sake, your sake.)
' Is the time come?   Is the time come? '   Ah, hush,
 no more: or my heart will break."

Pretty Kathie, closer pressing, into that face in
 silence peers:
There they fall, the sunset showers, the far-off,
 idle, eternal tears.

"BECAUSE NO MAN HATH HIRED US"

S. Matt. xx. 7.

I

ILL I, that am a soldier born, can find
    Some war so worthy, I may pledge it straight
    Unto my dear and virgin sword for mate,
Who now lies cloistered in her sheath behind,
Must I ride thus in vain; and on my mind
    The torment and the thirst of glory wait,
    And never cause with zeal inviolate
Be strong enough my haughty youth to bind.
Ah, readier men-at-arms! beneath the trees
Where shepherd-meek, I bear mine altered part,
    And watch the charge far off, and think with awe:
I have seen higher, holier things than these,
And therefore must to these refuse my heart,[1] —
    That heavenly pride forbids my hand to draw.

II

Though all your flags sweep stormily in air,
And thousand hoofs are whirling fiery seed,

[1] Τὸ καλόν : Arthur Hugh Clough.

48

The quiet forest hides my folly, freed
From good in reach, nor leagued to aught more
      fair.
This is my camp of tears, and doubt, and care,
Where I who long to fight may soothe my greed,
Full of sad liberty ; and if indeed
The One I lack came hither unaware, —
If sudden stood beside the saddle-bow
The Outcast of all time and every land,
With head drooped like the lily's parching cup,
I dare to dream that I my King should know,
And lean to kiss, within that wounded Hand,
My only use, my honors, folded up.

AN OUTDOOR LITANY

THE spur is red upon the briar,
   The sea-kelp whips the wave ashore;
   The wind shakes out the colored fire
   From lamps a-row on the sycamore;
The tanager, with flitting note,
Shows to wild heaven his wedding-coat;
The mink is busy; herds again
Go hillward in the honeyed rain;
The midges meet. I cry to Thee
Whose heart
Remembers each of these: Thou art
My God who hast forgotten me.

Bright from the mast, a scarf unwound,
The lined gulls in the offing ride;
Along an edge of marshy ground
The shad-bush enters like a bride.
Yon little clouds are washed of care
That climb the blue New England air,
And almost merrily withal
The tree-frog plays at evenfall
His oboe in a mossy tree.
So too,

Am I not Thine?   Arise, undo
This fear Thou hast forgotten me.

Happy the vernal rout that come
To their due offices to-day,
And strange, if in Thy mercy's sum,
Excluded man alone decay.
I ask no triumph, ask no joy,
Save leave to live, in law's employ.
As to a weed, to me but give
Thy sap! lest aye inoperative
Here in the Pit my strength shall be:
And still
Help me endure the Pit, until
Thou wilt not have forgotten me.

VIRGO GLORIOSA, MATER AMAN-
TISSIMA

VINES branching stilly
    Shade the open door,
    In the house of Zion's Lily,
    Cleanly and poor.
O brighter than wild laurel
The Babe bounds in her hand,
The King, who for apparel
Hath but a swaddling-band,
And sees her heavenlier smiling than stars in His
        command !

    Soon, mystic changes
    Part Him from her breast,
    Yet there awhile He ranges
    Gardens of rest :
    Yea, she the first to ponder
    Our ransom and recall,
    Awhile may rock Him under
    Her young curls' fall,
Against that only sinless love-loyal heart of all.

    What shall inure Him
    Unto the deadly dream,

When the tetrarch shall abjure Him,
The thief blaspheme,
And scribe and soldier jostle
About the shameful Tree,
And even an Apostle
Demand to touch and see ? —
But she hath kissed her Flower where the Wounds
     are to be.

FOUR COLLOQUIES

TO H. P. K.

I. THE SEARCH

WHY dost thou hide from these
Out along the hills halloaing?
Why hast forbade
Thy face, O goddess! to thy votaries?"

" *Unasking and unknowing*
Is he whom I make glad,
Like Dian grandly going
To the sleeping shepherd-lad.
Men that pursue learn not
To follow is my lot."

" Happiness, secret one,
Heartbeat of the April weather,
Where art thou found?
Tell; lest I err too, yonder in the sun."

" *Call in thine eye from ether,*
Thy feet from far ground;
Seek Honor in this heather,

54

With austere purples wound.
Serve her : she will reveal
Me, hound-like, at thy heel."

II. FACT AND THE MYSTIC

" Good-morrow, Symbol." — " *Call me not*
   The name I neither love nor merit."
    — " That grave eternal name inherit,
Thine ever, though all men forgot."

" *Mistake me not ; secure and free,*
   From rock to rock my falchion passes :
   But Symbols trail through gray morasses
The tattered shows of faëry."

" My Symbol thou, of phantom blood,
   With starlight from thy temples raying ;
   Along thy floated body playing
Are withering wings, and wings in bud."

" *Alas, thine eye with clay is sealed."*
    — " Symbol, before the clay's denial,
   While yet I had a god's espial,
I saw thee in a solar field ! "

" *Nay : I am Fact."* — " Then lose thy praise ;
   And lest to-day no song behoove thee,
   Lest mine impeach thee, or reprove thee,
Ah, Symbol, Symbol ! go thy ways."

III. THE POET'S CHART

"Where shall I find my light?""

" *Turn from another's track:*
Whether for gain or lack,
Love but thy natal right.
Cease to follow withal,
Though on thine up-led feet
Flakes of the phosphor fall.
Oracles overheard
Are never again for thee,
Nor at a magian's knee
Under the hemlock tree,
Burns the illumining word."

"Whence shall I take my law?""

" *Neither from sires nor sons,*
Nor the delivered ones,
Holy, invoked with awe.
Rather, dredge the divine
Out of thine own poor dust,
Feebly to speak and shine.
Schools shall be as they are:
Be thou truer, and stray
Alone, intent, and away,
In a savage wild to obey
A dim primordial star."

IV. OF THE GOLDEN AGE

" Recall for me, recall
  The time more true and ample;
  The world whereon I trample,
  How tortuous and small!
  Behold, I tire of all.

Once, gods in jeweled mail
Through greenwood ways invited;
There now the moon is blighted,
And mosses long and pale
On lifeless cedars trail."

" *Child, keep this good unrest :*
  But give to thine own story
  Simplicity with glory ;
  To greatness dispossessed,
  Dominion of thy breast.

In abstinence, in pride,
Thou, who from Folly's boldest
Thy sacred eye withholdest,
Another morn shalt ride
At Agamemnon's side."

SANCTUARY

HIGH above hate I dwell :
O storms ! farewell.
Though at my sill your daggered
thunders play,
Lawless and loud to-morrow as to-day,
To me they sound more small
Than a young fay's footfall :
Soft and far-sunken, forty fathoms low
In Long Ago,
And winnowed into silence on that wind
Which takes wars like a dust, and leaves but love
behind.

Hither Felicity
Doth climb to me,
And bank me in with turf and marjoram
Such as bees lip, or the new-weanèd lamb ;
With golden barberry-wreath,
And bluets thick beneath ;
One grosbeak, too, mid apple-buds a guest
With bud-red breast,
Is singing, singing ! All the hells that rage
Float less than April fog below our hermitage.

RANGE and olive and glossed bay-tree,
And air of the evening out at sea,
And out at sea, on the steep warm
    stone,
A little bare diver poising alone.

Flushed from the cool of Sicilian waves,
Flushed as the coral in clean sea-caves,
" I am ! " he cries to his glorying heart,
And unto he knows not what : " THOU art ! "

He leaps, he shines, he sinks, he is gone :
He will climb to the golden ledge anon.
Perfecter rite can none employ,
When the god of the isle is good to a boy.

THE INNER FATE: A CHORUS

NOT weak with eld
The stars beheld
Proud Persia coming to her doom ;
Not battle-broke, nor tempest-tossed,
The long luxurious galleys lost
Their souls at Actium.

Not outer arts
Of hostile hearts
Persuaded him of France to be
The wreckage of his wars at last,
The orphan of the kingdoms, cast
Upon the mothering sea.

Man evermore doth work his will,
And evermore the gods are still,
Applauding him alone who stands
Too just for heaven-accusing groans,
And in his house of havoc owns
The doing of his hands ;
Transgressor, yet divinely taught
To suffer all, blaspheming naught,

When fair-begun must foul conclude :
Himself progenitor of death,
Who breeds, within, the only breath
Can kill beatitude.

OF JOAN'S YOUTH

I WOULD unto my fair restore
A simple thing :
The flushing cheek she had before !
Out-velveting
No more, no more
By Severn shore,
The carmine grape, the moth's auroral wing.

Ah, say how winds in flooding grass
Unmoor the rose ;
Or guileful ways the salmon pass
To sea, disclose ;
For so, alas,
With Love, alas,
With fatal, fatal Love a girlhood goes.

BY THE TRUNDLE-BED

TO M. M. R.

MOST love, be never beyond Love's
    calling!
For this I claim of you, strong heart,
    sweet
As fontal water in Arden falling,
As first-mown hay in the April heat:

To tend from heaven, to rear, to harden,
And bring to bloom in the outer cold,
Our daffodil bud of a walled-in garden,
Our son that is like you, and six years old;

And lest his worth be the worth unreal,
To ward him not from the mortal blast,
But suffer your own, through a long ordeal,
Verily like you to be at the last,

And hear men murmur, if so he merit
In your old place with your look to arise:
"The sign of a saved soul who can inherit? —
You have earned, O King! those beautiful eyes."

THE ACKNOWLEDGMENT

SINCE first I knew it our divine employ
   To beat beyond the reach of soiling
      care,
   As at Philippi, well of doom aware,
The Prætor called and heard the singing boy;
Since first my soul so jealous was of joy,
   That any facile linden-bloom in air,
   Or fall of water on a wildwood stair,
Annulled for her all dragging dull annoy;
Though word of thanks I lacked, though, dumb, I
      smiled
Long, long, at such august amends up-piled,
   Let this the debt redeem : that when Ye drop
Death's aloe-leaf within my honeyed cup,
   On thoughtful knee your much-beholden child,
Immortals ! unto You will drink it up.

ARBORICIDE

A WORD of grief to me erewhile :
We have cut the oak down, in our isle.

And I said : " Ye have bereaven
The song-thrush and the bee,
And the fisher-boy at sea
Of his sea-mark in the even ;
And gourds of cooling shade, to lie
Within the sickle's sound ;
And the old sheep-dog's loyal eye
Of sleep on duty's ground ;
And poets of their tent
And quiet tenement.
Ah, impious ! who so paid
Such fatherhood, and made
Of murmurous immortality a cargo and a trade."

For the hewn oak a century fair,
A wound in earth, an ache in air.

And I said : " No pillared height
With a summer daïs over,
Where a dryad fled her lover

Through the long arcade of light;
Nor 'neath Arcturus rolleth more,
Since the loud leaves are gone,
Between the shorn cliff and the shore,
Pan's organ antiphon.
Some nameless envy fed
This blow at grandeur's head :
Some breathed reproach o'erdue,
Degenerate men, ye drew !
Then, for his too plain heavenliness, our Socrates
        ye slew."

CHARISTA MUSING

LOVELESS, on the marge of a sunny
    cornfield,
    Rapt in sudden revery while thou
    standest,
Like the sheaves, in beautiful Doric yellow
Clad to the ankle,

Oft to thee with delicate hasty footstep
So I steal, and suffer because I find thee
Inly flown, and only a fallen feather
Left of my darling.

Give me back thy wakening breath, thy ringlets
Fragrant as the vine of the bean in blossom,
And those eyes of violet dusk and daylight
Under sea-water,

Eyes too far away, and too full of longing !
Yes : and go not heavenward where I lose thee,
Go not, go not whither I cannot follow,
Being but earthly.

Willing swallow poisèd upon my finger,
Little wild-wing ever from me escaping,
For the care thou art to me, I thy lover
Love thee, and fear thee.

THE PERFECT HOUR

BE it on my blazon shown
How I fought the fiends alone,
Ere I rose to this content,
Open, true, magnificent.

My heart from the underworld
Rides the bright sea-foam upcurled;
My heart suns in air between
Medlar-pear and nectarine;

Terrors run to me at dawn
Tamer than the velvet fawn;
Not to me hath Love denied
His great star of eventide.

Fate, where is thy splintered spear
Met me in the tourney year?
Once thou wert in overthrow,
Then I laughed, and let thee go.

Wouldst thou yet make sport of me,
Find me kingly, fervent, free!
Though there come the foreordained,
In thy city have I not reigned?

69

DEO OPTIMO MAXIMO

ALL else for use, one only for desire ;
    Thanksgiving for the good, but thirst
      for Thee :
Up from the best, whereof no man need
      tire,
    Impel thou me.

Delight is menace, if Thou brood not by,
Power a quicksand, Fame a gathering jeer.
Oft as the morn, (though none of earth deny
These three are dear,)

Wash me of them, that I may be renewed,
Nor wall in clay mine agonies and joys :
O close my hand upon Beatitude !
Not on her toys.

70

IN TIME OF TROUBLE

BELIEVE the word our gentle augur
   spake :
  Sweet are the uses of adversity,
  Sweet ever ; and in naught so sweet as
   this :
That though the heavens be barred, if we but hold
An equal, quiet, will-illumined mind,
Such greatness in us, laborless, must win
Great answers : cheer from all created things,
And interchange of love by natural right
With the high few, a kinship not of clay.
Be these thy present comfort !   Like a man
Who tends a watchlight on the hills alone
At Childermas, (and through a night so cold,
The red clots of the rowan-berry twirl
Incorporate with a small stiff cone of ice,
And the wind breaks his flail, and swineherds hear
Outside, the pine-boles crack with frost i' the
  heart,)
Thou shalt, ere long, upon a distant peak
Descry a doubted smoke, a likelier spark,
A shadow shot across a glare, and then
Two spurts of flame that bare the under sea ;

And climb, by much and more of certitude,
To praising God some other even as thou
Beneath his natal star himself maintains,
And in salute of souls coördinate,
There, till he perish, guards his lineal fire.

AN ESTRAY

WELL we know, not ever here is a footing for thy dream :
Thou art sick for horse and spear beside an Asian stream,

For the hearth-smoke in the wild, for the goatherd's stave,
For a beauty far exiled, a belief within its grave.

While another sky and ground orb thy strange remembering,
And no world of mortal bound is the master of thy wing,

Canst thou yet thy fate forgive, that the godhead in thy breast
Has this life at least to live as a force in rhythmic rest,

As a seed that bides the hour of obscureness and decay,
Being troth of flower to flower down the long dynastic day ?

Child whom elder airs enfold, who hast greatness
       to maintain
Where heroic hap of old may return and shine
       again,

As too oft across thy heart flits the too familiar
       light,
How alarms of love upstart at the token quick and
       slight !

Lest captivity be o'er, lest thou glide away, and so
From our tents of Nevermore strike the trail of
       Long Ago.

THROUGH all the evening,
    All the virginal long evening,
    Down the blossomed aisle of April it
        is dread to walk alone;
For there the intangible is nigh, the lost is ever-
    during;
And who would suffer again beneath a too divine
    alluring,
Keen as the ancient drift of sleep on dying faces
    blown?

Yet in the valley,
At a turn of the orchard alley,
When a wild aroma touched me in the moist and
    moveless air,
Like breath indeed from out Thee, or as airy ves-
    ture round Thee,
Then was it I went faintly, for fear I had nearly
    found Thee,
O hidden, O perfect, O desired! the first and the
    final Fair.

TO THE OUTBOUND REPUBLIC:
MDCCCXCVIII

AMERICA, bride of Change!
Thy cloistral hour is done;
Thy shy and innocent foot
Is white on the stranger's stair:
Unto what end? — Beloved!
I have heard thee sigh.

As the heliotrope in the dusk
Close under, but unespied,
Delivers one slow breath,
Pained, poignant-sweet,
Into the neutral air,
Because she inly feels
At some light shock of a bud
That would issue forth, and expand,
How coronals fall, and old
Dear purples wither away;
(While the friendly leaves o'erhead
Moan, and the redwing there
Aches in his delicate sleep;)
Even so,
Freedom's exempted flower!
In the rhythm, the interplay

Of the terrors of budding life
Or death,
I have heard thee sigh.

As the clear mid-channel wave,
That under a Lammas dawn
Her orient lanthorn held
Steady and beautiful,
Through the trance of the sunken tide,
Sudden leaps up, and spreads
Her signal round the sea :
Time, time !
Time to awake ; to arm ;
To scale the difficult shore !
Even so,
Thou Heart of the dual deep,
Ere the plash of the onset came,
In the vortices
I have heard thee sigh.

What if now
Thou failest, our saint, our star !
Between thy Father's tomb,
And the throne of the glittering world,
The febrile world,
Calling,
Ah, Child ! (have I lived too long ?)
I have heard thee sigh.

ODE FOR A MASTER MARINER
ASHORE

THERE in his room, whene'er the moon
 looks in,
 And silvers now a shell, and now a
 fin,
And o'er his chart glides like an argosy,
Quiet and old sits he.
Danger ! he hath grown homesick for thy smile.
Where hidest thou the while, heart's boast,
Strange face of beauty sought and lost,
Star-face that lured him out from boyhood's isle ?

Blown clear from dull indoors, his dreams behold
Night-water smoke and sparkle as of old,
The taffrail lurch, the sheets triumphant toss
Their phosphor-flowers across.
Towards ocean's either rim the long-exiled
Wears on, till stunted cedars throw
A lace-like shadow over snow,
Or tropic fountains wash their agates wild.

Awhile, play up and down the briny spar
Odors of Surinam and Zanzibar,

Till blithely thence he ploughs, in visions new,
The Labradorian blue ;
All homeless hurricanes about him break ;
The purples of spent day he sees
From Samos to the Hebrides,
And drowned men dancing darkly in his wake.

Where the small deadly foam-caps, well descried,
Top, tier on tier, the hundred-mountained tide, ·
Away, and far away, his pride is borne,
Riding the noisy morn,
Plunges, and preens her wings, and laughs to
        know
The helm and tightening halyards still
Follow the urging of his will,
And scoff at sullen earth a league below.

Mischance hath barred him from his heirdom high,
And shackled him with many an inland tie,
And of his only wisdom made a jibe
Amid an alien tribe :
No wave abroad but moans his fallen state.
The trade-wind ranges now, the trade-wind roars !
Why is it on a yellowing page he pores ?
Ah, why this hawser fast to a garden gate ?

Thou friend so long withdrawn, so deaf, so dim,
Familiar Danger, O forget not him !

Repeat of thine evangel yet the whole
Unto his subject soul,
Who suffers no such palsy of her drouth,
Nor hath so tamely worn her chain,
But she may know that voice again,
And shake the reefs with answer of her mouth.

O give him back, before his passion fail,
The singing cordage and the hollow sail,
And level with those aged eyes let be
The bright unsteady sea;
And move like any film from off his brain
The pasture wall, the boughs that run
Their evening arches to the sun,
The hamlet spire across the sown champaign;

And on the shut space and the trivial hour,
Turn the great floods! and to thy spousal bower,
With rapt arrest and solemn loitering,
Him whom thou lovedst, bring:
That he, thy faithful one, with praising lip,
Not having, at the last, less grace
Of thee than had his roving race,
Sum up his strength to perish with a ship.

THE RECRUIT

SO much to me is imminent:
   To leave Revolt that is my tent,
   And Failure, chosen for my bride,

And into life's highway be gone,
Ere yet Creation marches on,
Obedient, jocund, glorified;

And last of things afoot, to know
How to be free is still to go
With glad concession, grave accord,

Nor longer, bond and imbecile,
Stand out against the gradual Will,
The guessed _Fall in !_ of God the Lord.

The Martyrs' Idyl first came out in the Christmas number, 1898, of Harper's Magazine. With the exception of that, of three poems taken from "England and Yesterday" (Grant Richards, London), and of one other, the contents of this volume appeared prior to 1896 in Harper's, The Century, The Cosmopolitan, The Independent, The Chap-Book, etc., to all of which thanks are due for the courteous permission to reprint.

ELECTROTYPED AND PRINTED
BY H. O. HOUGHTON AND CO.

𝕿𝖍𝖊 𝕽𝖎𝖛𝖊𝖗𝖘𝖎𝖉𝖊 𝕻𝖗𝖊𝖘𝖘

CAMBRIDGE, MASS., U. S. A.